growing a masterpiece

Frederik Meijer Gardens & Sculpture Park

growing a masterpiece

PHOTOGRAPHY

William J. Hebert

TEXT

Alan Rosas

POETRY

Patricia Clark

Linda Nemec Foster

Dan Gerber

Miriam Pederson

Rodney Torreson

Robert VanderMolen

Frederik Meijer Gardens & Sculpture Park

Grand Rapids, Michigan

This book has been published on the occasion of the tenth anniversary of Frederik Meijer Gardens & Sculpture Park, April 20, 2005.

Frederik Meijer Gardens & Sculpture Park is a 125-acre botanical garden and sculpture park whose signature is the dynamic interrelationship of horticulture and sculpture. It is our mission to promote the enjoyment, understanding, and appreciation of gardens, sculpture, the natural environment, and the arts. We are dedicated to delivering an enlightening, imaginative, and engaging cultural experience that will stimulate the senses and nourish the mind, body, and spirit.

First published in the United States of America in 2005 by

Frederik Meijer Gardens & Sculpture Park
1000 East Beltline NE
Grand Rapids, Michigan 49525

in part through the generosity of the Meijer Foundation.

Library of Congress Control Number: 2005920933
ISBN: 0-9712034-5-8

Principal photography by William J. Hebert. Additional photography: pages 54 and 56 (upper right), courtesy of Frederik Meijer Gardens & Sculpture Park; page 56 (lower left), courtesy of Johnny Quirin.

Copyright credits for works of art can be found on page 104.

Editor: E. Jane Connell
Project director: Sally Littlefair Zarafonetis
Designed by Jeff Wincapaw
Color separations by iocolor, Seattle
Produced by Marquand Books, Inc., Seattle
    www.marquand.com
Printed and bound by CS Graphics Pte., Ltd., Singapore

<< A bright bed of black-eyed Susans, *Rudbeckia fulgida* var. *sullivantii* 'Goldsturm', are the foreground of Michigan's largest tropical conservatory standing tall against the sunset.

A bumblebee works the delicate flowers of Gaura, *Gaura lindheimeri* 'Whirling Butterflies'.

contents

Foreword

Travel the world and you may be hard pressed to find another place that celebrates the marriage of culture and horticulture with such dedication as the Gardens. Comments from more than three million guests who have visited since our opening in April 1995 speak of "pleasant surprises," "exceeded expectations," and "beyond our imagination."

The early seeds of this signature union of art and nature were planted by leaders of many of the area's major garden clubs, who dreamed of developing a botanical garden that would serve the West Michigan community. One of these botanical leaders made contact with successful businessman Frederik Meijer, who during this same time—many say in a humorous way—was bitten by the sculpture bug. Meijer had collected a significant number of sculptures, but did not have an appropriate place to share them with others. He was intrigued by the notion of creating a botanical garden and infusing it with a significant sculptural presence.

To this end, Fred Meijer and his wife Lena generously donated 125 acres of land, their entire sculpture collection, and a major gift to the initial $13 million capital campaign, setting the roots to grow what is now nationally known as Frederik Meijer Gardens & Sculpture Park. Much of what the Gardens has become in its first decade can be attributed to the Meijer family's commitment to quality development and design, artistic significance, and accessibility to everyone, achieving a unique experience that is welcoming and friendly.

The Gardens quickly became—and continues to be—a source of community pride, reflecting the grassroots support of West Michigan. Hundreds of volunteers teamed up with a creative professional staff, a loyal membership grew rapidly, and visitation increased dramatically. The popularity of the Gardens skyrocketed, and it became one of the top attractions in the state of Michigan. A master plan, generated with input from the community, members, and supporters, has guided the aggressive expansion of the Gardens through its first decade. Based on survey results, the Gardens has become a true reflection of what the greater community desired of its botanical garden and sculpture park.

Five of the seven major theme areas represented in the master plan are completed or substantially under way. The Gardens of Innovation, the Sculpture Park, the Cultural Arts Center, Michigan's Farm Garden, and the Lena Meijer

Children's Garden have been inspiring, educating, and entertaining guests throughout the seasons. The future holds exciting plans for the development of Gardens of the World, an array of internationally themed gardens, and America's Backyard, a group of innovative home idea gardens with a strong residential focus.

The Gardens has an intrinsic appeal to people of all ages. Whether it is an elementary-school class on a field trip or college-level art students studying the sculpture collection, the Gardens lives its educational mission every day of the year. Adult tour groups choose us as a must-see destination when traveling through the area. The new Children's Garden, positioned at the heart of the outdoor complex, has introduced an interactive learning landscape that has an amazing, fun magnetism for kids of all ages in all four seasons.

The Gardens has become a place where special memories are created as people celebrate milestones in their lives. From weddings in the lush, tropical forest in the Lena Meijer Conservatory to one-of-a-kind special events in the Grand Room, the Gardens continues to grow in popularity as a location for people to gather and socialize.

The ongoing acquisition and presentation of distinguished works of modern and contemporary sculpture have a somewhat youthful history here. The interior temporary exhibition galleries opened in September 2000 with the visionary work of Richard Hunt. The gallery complex continues to showcase significant works by internationally celebrated artists including Anthony Caro, Dale Chihuly, Mark di Suvero, Henry Moore, Claes Oldenburg and Coosje van Bruggen, Pablo Picasso, Auguste Rodin, and George Segal.

The Sculpture Park, where the majority of the permanent sculpture collection is located, opened to the public in May 2002. It has captured the attention of the art world with thoughtfully conceived installations of major works by an ever-expanding roster of artists including Magdalena Abakanowicz, Jonathan Borofsky, Louise Bourgeois, Deborah Butterfield, Alexander Calder, Keith Haring, Barbara Hepworth, Alexander Liberman, Jacques Lipchitz, Aristide Maillol, Henry Moore, Louise Nevelson, Arnaldo Pomodoro, and George Rickey. Thirty acres of contemplative vistas, open fields, intimate wooded alcoves, peaceful waterways, and meandering pathways provide an exceptional natural stage for this artistic legacy. Whether illuminated by a stunning summer sunset or frosted by wintry weather, the sculpture is at home and in harmony with its outdoor environment throughout the seasons.

Botanically, the 15,000-square-foot, five-story Lena Meijer Conservatory is the largest tropical conservatory in the state of Michigan. Each year in March and April, the Conservatory presents the nation's largest free-flying tropical butterfly exhibit. The magic of thousands of exotic tropical butterflies from around the world thrills Gardens guests with memorable experiences while presenting important concepts of environmental sensitivities and stewardship within the global garden. With "grand openings" every day of the year, the botanical collections and their sensual impact are part of the allure of the Gardens. Orchids and bromeliads, cacti and succulents, carnivorous plants and dramatic seasonal displays presented throughout the changing seasons are the horticultural hallmarks of the Gardens.

The architecture of the Conservatory, and indeed of all of the Gardens' structures, is engineered to connect art and nature in compelling ways that provide an additional basis for study and inspiration. Symbols of nature and seasonal attributes have been incorporated into the design of the facilities as eye-catching and educational details. A leaf motif, for example, is prevalent throughout the interior and exterior of the main building; its imagery is found in the pavement, wall and floor coverings, fabrics, railings, and signs.

The Gardens' 1,800-person outdoor amphitheater has become a popular major entertainment venue in West Michigan. Our stage has welcomed outstanding performing artists including Judy Collins, Charlie Daniels, Bela Fleck, Art Garfunkel, Arlo Guthrie, the Indigo Girls, B. B. King, and Branford Marsalis. The spotlight is shared throughout the summer concert season with a balanced mix of featured local musicians as well as the Grand Rapids Symphony.

When former president Jimmy Carter visited the Gardens in 2002, on the morning of the first anniversary of September 11, he departed refreshed, encouraged, and inspired. This oasis of serenity, beauty, and welcoming friendliness, a soothing contrast to the fateful events of the year before, impressed the gentleman from Plains. As he left the Gardens, he remarked, "You truly have a national treasure here."

Shadows fall across a wall of multicolored quarried limestone at the Gardens' entrance.

The Lena Meijer Conservatory is reflected in the Wetlands Pond.

Dietrich Klinge's *Grosser Trefree* in snow.

With special recognition and appreciation to Fred and Lena Meijer, this anniversary book is dedicated to the people who have contributed in ways great and small to the treasure that is Frederik Meijer Gardens & Sculpture Park. As we continue to devote ourselves to delivering an enlightening, imaginative, and engaging cultural experience that will stimulate the senses and nourish the mind, body, and spirit, we embrace the future from strengths and successes rooted in our first ten years.

R. Brent Dennis
Executive Director, Frederik Meijer Gardens & Sculpture Park

These pages provide a passage to the wonders of the Gardens. They compress the changing seasons and hours of pleasure into something you can hold in your hand.

Pages of Memory

>> Red blooms of Crocosmia, *Crocosmia* 'Lucifer', reach through the garden.

A red-winged blackbird in flight.

Every time you come through the gates, you will see something unexpected: surprising vistas, sounds, and flavors changed by weather, menu, growth cycle, or entertainment schedule.

Every visit offers a gift to the spirit—the dart of a bird, the rise of a seedling, the arc of bright metal against a stormy sky, the refrain of a song settling on a hillside. This unique amalgam of nature, sculpture, and performance is in dynamic flux. Come and let your senses be rewarded.

Living things are in a constant state of change

A Stage for Change and Permanence

Traditionally, many sculptors choose durable materials, like bronze, marble, and steel, that are meant to convey an idea for generations to come. In the Sculpture Park, the works of art, set in particular locations, are framed by the living plants, the skittering clouds, the movement of the sun across the sky. This contrast of permanence and change is powerfully emotive. Yet despite the notion of changelessness, the sculptures do not look

whereas art is often an attempt at some degree of permanence.

the same from day to day. They are bare or snow covered, shadowless or heavily shadowed, reflecting the green of spring, the gray of winter, or the amber and orange of fall. Some sculptures use water or wind as components. The sculpture becomes natural, and nature becomes sculptural.

spring

<< The Joe Pye flower, *Eupatorium maculatum* 'Gateway', stretches tall in the Jennifer C. Groot New American Garden.

Daffodils, *Narcissus* sp., usher in spring at the Gardens.

Canada goose and baby goslings make their home at the Gardens.

Purple cranesbills, *Geranium × magnificum,* and golden tickseed, *Coreopsis verticillata* 'Zagreb', brighten up a hillside.

Spring is birth. There is a particular yellow-green in spring that you see at no other time of year.

It is an iridescent signal of new life that entices you to notice fragile structures emerging from the ground.

A flurry of tulips in the Leslie E. Tassell English Perennial & Bulb Garden.

The soil has a different smell. The sun has shifted, and the shadows are shorter and more sharply defined. After hibernating for months of winter, the crisp spring air and pools of sun-warmth make the freedom of the trails at the Gardens irresistible. The grass is wet, but there is grass, and you can sit in it and happily suffer a damp bottom until another walk dries you out.

Whimsical figures of Joseph Kinnebrew's *The Visitation* rise above Hoffius Hill with its massing of ornamental grasses.

The Sculpture Park Waterfall
is a compelling backdrop for
Mimmo Paladino's *Tana*.

Daylily
Hemerocallis
lilio-asphodelus
Liliaceae
E. Asia, Japan

Spring flowers jostle for attention in the Leslie E. Tassell English Perennial & Bulb Garden.

Morning dew is caught on the floral lace of coral bells, *Heuchera* sp.

In early spring, rhododendrons, *Rhododendron* spp., bloom boldly in the Gwen Frostic Woodland Shade Garden.

Tulips in the Leslie E. Tassell
English Perennial & Bulb Garden.

sweet vernal grass

Patricia Clark

Between here and the lake, the purple clover bloomed
with meadow buttercups and sweet vernal grass.

Fountain grass,
*Pennisetum
alopecuroides.*

A lawn of sorts, a semi-circle of gravel drive,
and then the wild, lapsed meadow into which

a pheasant disappeared. The hunting spaniel came
nose down, traversing and sniffing. I thought

any moment it would flush out, with a cry.
The taller field waved and rippled in wind,

with floating sweet-grass, soft rush, sneezewort.
And dark pools floated underneath the trees—

Scot's pine and a lone redwood to the east. The dog
caught nothing. The pheasant ruffled down in its lair

among tufted forget-me-not, the marsh foxtail
and marigold, and skullcap, too. Down the lane

the spaniel headed home. A mayfly, green
and drifting, sailed by into the second half

of its life, each hour seeming long, and enough.

A tree nymph, *Idea leuconoe.*

A banded orange, *Dryadula phaetusa.*

Spring is also the time for other kinds of new life.

Butterflies Bloom

We have all seen butterflies from a distance, but in the Lena Meijer Conservatory during the annual butterfly event, they emerge from the papery skins of their chrysalides by the thousands. Here, butterflies are our intimates, standing tiptoe on nearby plants and begging to be admired, to be seen from a few inches. Each one is a miracle, with forms and designs in brilliant colors painted on the minute scales of their wings.

These beautiful creatures float and swim around us in the dense air

occupying the unused space that once was just a medium for sunshine and humid warmth. Unanchored and unfettered, these bits of fluttering color are like winged flowers that are unafraid to meet us. The meetings are gracious. Even energetic, giggling children stop and move with extreme and gentle care, feeling honored by the trust of these fragile creatures.

A tropical swallowtail, *Parides iphidamas*. A clipper, *Parthenos sylvia*. An orange-barred sulphur, *Phoebis philea*.

This is a place where all five senses are celebrated and where the deeper intellect is invigorated. There is science here, but science presented gracefully, seamlessly, effortlessly. You can learn the Latin name of a plant, the breeding habits of a butterfly, or the way a sundial relates shadows to time. The lessons learned are almost accidental, a by-product of immersion in a world of wonder.

A Place Where Knowledge Grows

The restless movement of koi
swimming in the Sculpture
Park Waterfall Pond.

>> A view of the
Lena Meijer
Conservatory
at dusk.

Number 26
by Hanneke
Beaumont.

summer

Sedum, *Sedum ellacombianum,* grows around stones in the Sculpture Park.

Canna lily, *Canna* sp.

some distance

Dan Gerber

>> A bee's-eye view of the seeds of a sunflower, *Helianthus* sp.

Sunflowers, *Helianthus* sp., in the Lena Meijer Children's Garden.

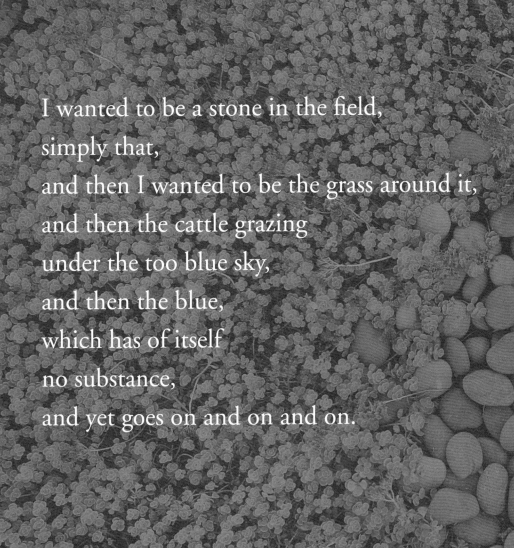

I wanted to be a stone in the field,
simply that,
and then I wanted to be the grass around it,
and then the cattle grazing
under the too blue sky,
and then the blue,
which has of itself
no substance,
and yet goes on and on and on.

Summer is freedom.

The kids are out of school. Everyone is ready for adventure.

High summer at the Gardens is when you are most aware of how informal this place can be.

Everyone is in shorts and sandals. Mothers carry babies in backpacks. Children run

while parents sit on shady benches. Visitors fill trams that roll down winding trails. A waterfall, a 1930s-era farm, and a building just for storytelling add to the mix of wondrous growing things and marvelous sculpture.

Red rose hips, *Rosa* 'Carmenetta', and chrysanthemum blooms, *Dendranthema zawadskii* 'Clara Curtis', bring color to a fading flower garden as the summer wanes.

Old-fashioned spider flowers, *Cleome hassleriana,* meet the theme of a replica of Lena Meijer's childhood home at Michigan's Farm Garden.

Standing 24 feet tall,
The American Horse at the
DeVos Van Andel Piazza is
enjoyed by many visitors.

Flower beds of the Ram's
Garden welcome visitors
at the Gardens' entrance.

Koi in the Sculpture Park
Waterfall Pond.

Plump zinnias, *Zinnia* 'Benary
Scarlet', provide cardinal color
all summer long.

A traditional Indian wedding
ceremony begins in the
Ram's Garden.

A summer concert at the Amphitheater.

Concert goers kick up their heels.

This is a place where children are welcome, where family memories are made. Families enjoy approachable art in nature settings. With its casual accessibility and aesthetic excellence, the Gardens delights children and offers adults many moments of transcendent beauty while walking the trails, places where the wind, sun, blossoming plants, and the dramatic sky create amazing backdrops for sculptural masterpieces.

A Family Place

Lively young enthusiasts
at the concert.

A child peeks out from Treehouse Village in the Children's Garden.

>> English ivy, *Hedera helix,* is manicured to clothe the topiary queen bee and her soldier companion in the Children's Garden.

Walk into the Children's Garden and see what makes the delightful sound—the long, slender, metal arms of the gamelans, gracefully turning in the wind and creating joyful sounds that are a perfect accompaniment to the laughter of children.

Watch the children as they enter through a mouse hole sized just for them. Off they go, exploring the winding paths that link a series of tree houses.

The Lena Meijer Children's Garden

Under their shaded roofs, viewports set at just the right height for curious

young eyes point out cleverly disguised displays of birds and other natural wonders.

An array of colorful tropical plants lends textural interest to the Children's Garden.

Down the slope, a quarry welcomes diggers and fossil hunters. Shovels are provided. Across the Great Lakes Plaza, a special sundial tells the time with each child's shadow.

Children love water. They launch toy boats that bob in kid-sized replicas of the Great Lakes. What color to choose, which boat to push on the sparkling water, these are the decisions of summer.

Children are endlessly fascinated with sailing boats on the kid-sized Great Lakes.

A budding archaeologist digs for fossils under the sand.

How the wildflowers danced our bare feet
through those paths
in search of friends or likely spots to build a fortress.

childhood's garden

Miriam Pederson

The Wetlands Overlook
in the Children's Garden.

The sky, its mouth as wide as time,
invited gazing from our hide-out in the field,
the clouds an entertainment, whether roly-poly penguins
or heavy beards of rain.
We hollered out the places we would go
when we grew up: Alcatraz! Timbuktu! Cocomo!
Places far away from here where palm trees
dropped their coconuts like hail
and butterflies and parrots
alighted on our heads and shoulders,
bright wings camouflaging our wiry frames.
Then, back in childhood's garden,
our games and ventures took us up the gnarled oak
and later down the cellar stairs
where we would stare at jars of sweet and tart
and sweet and sour of seasons past,
wondering how this harvest would taste upon our tongues.

fall

As one ventures at twilight
In late October, like a child
Except for the guilt of time,
How everything is alright,

bark

Robert VanderMolen

<< Red maples, *Acer rubrum,* are the first to signal autumn to the Gardens' woodlands.

A collage of autumn leaves.

The brilliant lemon yellows of the sugar maple, *Acer saccharum,* are highlighted by its dark limbs and trunk.

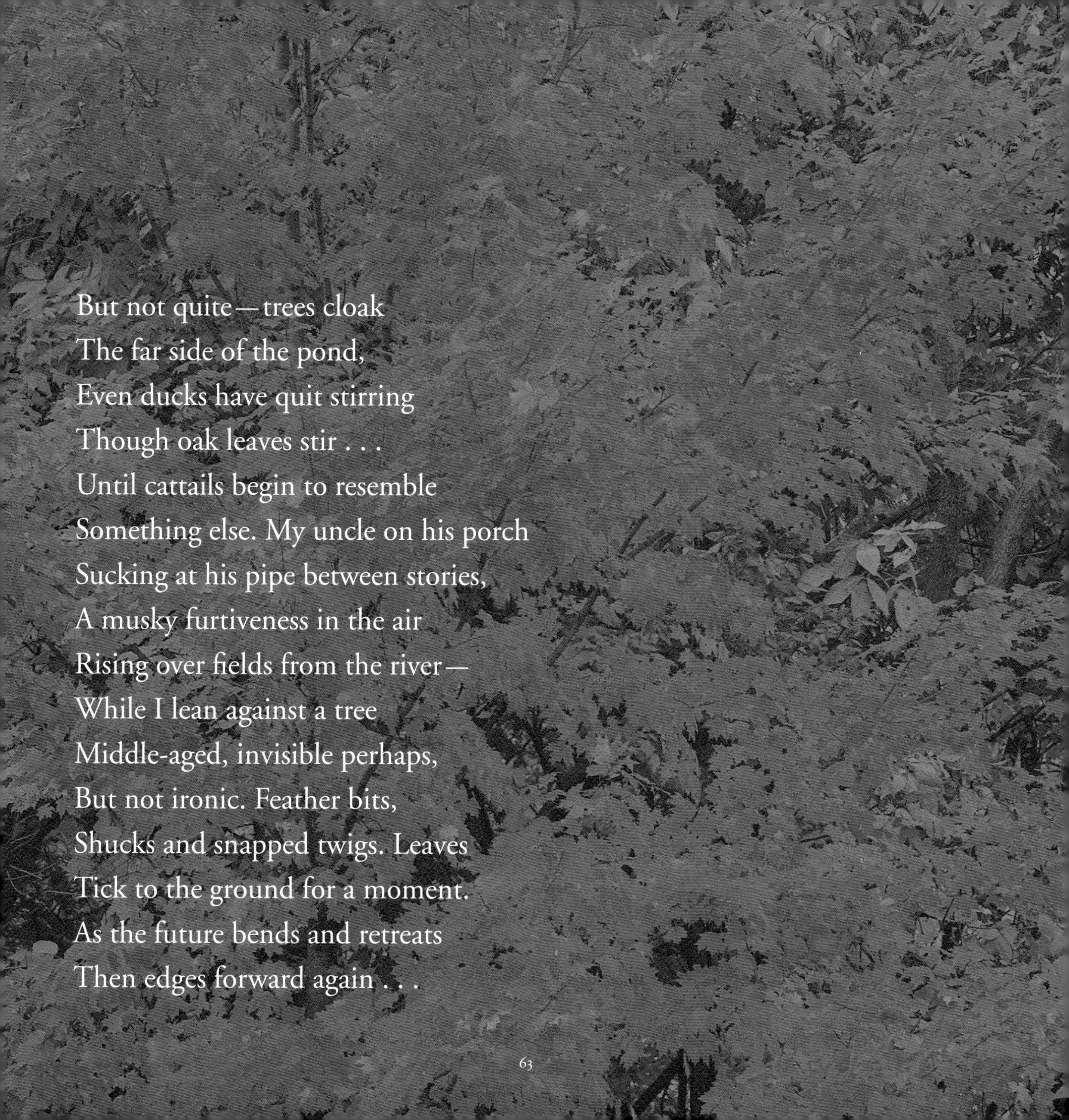

But not quite—trees cloak
The far side of the pond,
Even ducks have quit stirring
Though oak leaves stir . . .
Until cattails begin to resemble
Something else. My uncle on his porch
Sucking at his pipe between stories,
A musky furtiveness in the air
Rising over fields from the river—
While I lean against a tree
Middle-aged, invisible perhaps,
But not ironic. Feather bits,
Shucks and snapped twigs. Leaves
Tick to the ground for a moment.
As the future bends and retreats
Then edges forward again . . .

Native hickory, elm, maple, and cherry leaves create a colorful collage on the forest floor.

The flowering dogwood tree, *Cornus florida*, colors up in the Gwen Frostic Woodland Shade Garden.

Fall is crunchy.

Cameras click everywhere during the magical weeks when the sugars in the leaves are triggered by a few cold nights, transforming greens into confetti party colors against a brilliant cerulean sky. Different trees become different colors. There are large leaves and small leaves, outer leaves in gaudy display and inner ones that remain green. Michigan has a great many tree species, and their brilliant colors are a perfect backdrop for sculptural art. The color and texture of oxidizing iron and painted steel are never more compelling than when presented against a Michigan fall's oranges, reds, and yellows.

The majestic steel sculpture *Scarlatti*, by Mark di Suvero,
commands a hillside of the Harry & Elin Doehne
Wildflower Meadow.

The golden bronze patina of *Disk in the Form of a Desert Rose*,
by Arnaldo Pomodoro, complements the surrounding fall colors.

Reflections of fall. Sweetspire shrubs, *Itea verginica* 'Little Henry', turn from green to red in the Glen of the Sculpture Park, where George Rickey's *Four Open Squares Horizontal Gyratory—Tapered* shimmers in the background. Auguste Rodin's *Eve* is silhouetted against a fiery red sugar maple, *Acer saccharum*.

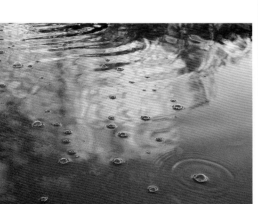

The flowering dogwood, *Cornus florida*, is one of the most reliable trees for beautiful autumn color.

Reflective qualities of water and stainless steel capture fall colors in George Rickey's *Four Open Squares Horizontal Gyratory—Tapered*.

A Haven for Art and Nature

It is wonderful to find this particular combination, this amazingly appropriate harmony of art and nature, assembled in just this way. The union of the arts with the natural environment is central to the mission of the Gardens. The art makes you see the plantings differently, and the plantings inform your appreciation of the art. Look up at the sensuous shapes of Dale Chihuly's roiling glass sculpture in the atrium. In the tropical conservatory nearby, glowing orchids are open on a stage of tangled vines. The comparison is compelling, two kinds of beauty in close proximity.

White fruit of native gray dogwood, *Cornus racemosa*, gives contrast to crimson foliage.

A lady slipper orchid, *Paphiopedilum* sp.

winter

<< Clusters of Washington hawthorn berries, *Crataegus phaenopyrum*, bring color to the frozen landscape.

A wolf from *Family of Wolves*, by Leonard Strekfus, peers out from a frosty mantle of snow.

Tree shadows play on snow-covered hills.

A fresh blanket of snow enhances the inward emotional bearing of Auguste Rodin's *Eve*.

Winter is pristine.

Snow purifies and simplifies.

White spruce, *Picea glauca*,
laden with snow.

It wraps the undulating hills with tiny sparkles

and reflective crystals like sequins on a white evening gown.

Barren hills and trees complement the look of weathered wood evoked in the bronze structure of *Cabin Creek* by Deborah Butterfield.

Ice and snow give new dimension to *Four Open Squares Horizontal Gyratory—Tapered* by George Rickey.

In this rolling, white, soft place are the sculptures—figures and shapes thrusting, reaching, growing out of the pillows of white. Every sculpture wears a white hat and a white coat in wonderful Michigan winters.

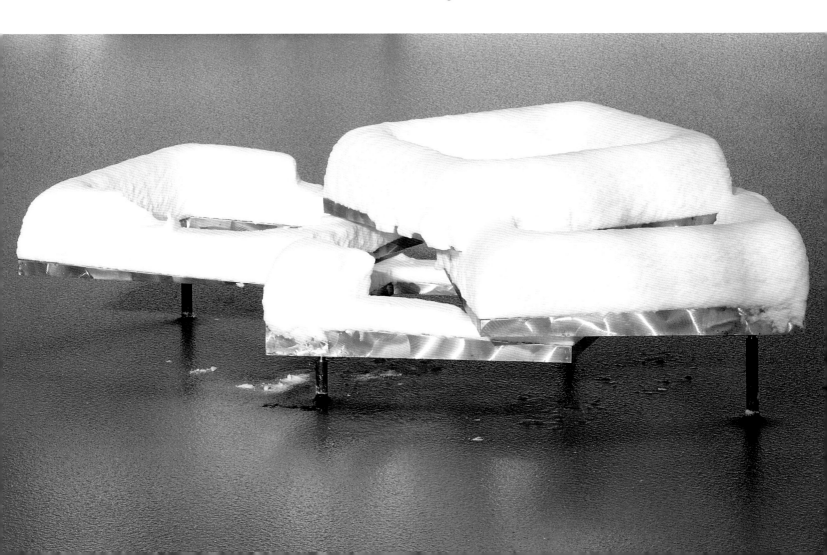

Before snow blowers conquered blizzards,
we fathomed such a horse—felt its complement,
a wind: robust, sculpted. On every street
we leaned against shovels, caught in our breath
the pride of ancients, then continued scooping
somehow closer to the horse.

da vinci's horse in snow

Rodney Torreson

The American Horse
by Nina Akamu.

When a snow-banked car spun wheels,
we'd rock it free, feel the equine pride
to lift as smartly our own right leg,
but knew at once how foolish we'd appear
taking such a step, next to memories
of a horse slipping past embarrassed, stranded cars
to deliver an expectant mother in her hour.
Or a story of a horse
pulling the full weight of the centuries,
then rearing, and in all its graceful heft
daring us to do the same. We fail before we begin,
smile and shake our heads, then later
in its shadow, pretend it was we who left.

Walk through the door and you feel the warmth and humidity; you smell the earth that anchors these magnificent living things.

The Lena Meijer Conservatory

What a delicious contrast it is to a cold winter's day! The Conservatory is outside and inside all at once. The soaring, crystalline space is vast and tropical, complete with the sound of a waterfall and the high-up motion of an occasional bird. Every inch is filled with life, a green crowd standing on either side of the narrow walking path. A plant as tall as a building reaches out with umbrella-sized

leaves and watches over the smaller plants. People stand in rapt delight, studying the beautiful inhabitants. Aficionados of garden rarities enjoy the color, the composition, and the texture, just as art collectors enjoy fine paintings.

The magnitude of the 15,000-square-foot Lena Meijer Conservatory, the largest tropical conservatory in Michigan, impresses visitors.

A flowering clerodendrom, *Clerodendrom speciosissimum,* blooms before a wall of palm leaves in the Lena Meijer Conservatory.

The fanged monkey pot, *Nepenthes bicalcarata,* awaits its next insect meal inside the Kenneth E. Nelson Carnivorous Plant House.

The Conservatory is just the beginning. Most of the world's ecosystems are represented. Walk to the nearby smaller indoor gardens: the Seasonal Display Greenhouse with changing exhibitions, the Victorian Garden with traditional plants and charming wrought iron fittings, the Arid Garden with its spiky population, and the bizarre Carnivorous Plant House with plants that attract, trap, and digest insects and other small creatures.

A Destination of Distinction

Many visitors are surprised to discover how remarkable the artworks are. In this informal environment, visitors can see many pieces made by artists of such renown that art history books feature their achievements. The Sculpture Park provides an extraordinary opportunity for visitors from around the world to enjoy internationally celebrated works of art showcased in both incredibly beautiful, natural settings and gracious interior galleries.

Alexander
Liberman's
Aria in winter.

Snowy hillsides reflect natural and man-made elements, such as this shadow of the Amphitheater.

This is a big place. Inside and outside, it is art and nature on a grand scale. As you enter the Gardens complex, you see something monumental and red, a forty-two-foot-tall sculpture called *Aria.* Alexander Liberman's sculpture, rising above the tree line, suggests the coiled tendrils of plants or calligraphic pen strokes or a thousand other things that are fun and curvy.

Big

The trails themselves are curvy, winding through softly rolling hills, beauty that goes on and on, shaded by oak, beech, and maple trees of a majestic size appropriate to this big place. Around one bend, you will find something so unexpectedly large that it stops you in your tracks—an enormous red trowel, its point embedded in the ground as if by an enormous gardener. At more than twenty-three feet high, this sculpture called *Plantoir,* by Claes Oldenburg and Coosje van Bruggen, compels you to take a fresh look at something you would normally hold in your hand. *Plantoir* makes you smile.

Then there are pieces that, although they are smaller in scale, are great in emotional power. *Grosser Trefree,* by Dietrich Klinge, is an enigmatic, primal symbol: a totemic, seated figure that seems to have been made before history, as if hewn from wood with an ax and then transformed by magic into bronze. *Grosser Trefree* sits on a block of stone, a timeless arbor deity made of metal yet showing the grain and texture of the wood of its origin, patterns in the beautiful, dark patina, a surface honoring the living trees that surround and envelop the space. The figure, straight backed, legs drawn up, has its arms in a continuous circle, the oldest symbol of life.

Perhaps the biggest things of all you find here are the big hearts and generosity of Fred and Lena Meijer . . . very big indeed.

Standing nearly 24 feet high, the colossal *Plantoir*, by Claes Oldenburg and Coosje van Bruggen, harbors a delicate dusting of snow.

The cracked, fissured bark is a feature of this massive 200-year-old sugar maple, *Acer saccharum*.

Blue herons are frequent
visitors at the Gardens.

A snow-covered *Grosser*
Trefree by Dietrich Klinge.

A Place of Continual Change

This is a living, changing place. Of course the plants are living and growing. The seasons are actors in the drama. Even the themes of the Gardens are in a state of evolution as areas are added and improved. There is always something new to see, exhibits of rare plants, celebrations and events. The Sculpture Park and galleries provide new art that challenges our precepts. The amphitheater stage reverberates with a varied roster of major names in entertainment. The Gardens is a destination with a panoply of offerings that nourish the soul and invite sampling again and again.

W hat can hope give us that is more perfect
than a new day? Above the mist-covered trees,
the solitary sun opens its shining eye
and dispels every inch of dark still lingering

our imagined lives

Linda Nemec Foster

Along the garden path, wispy
plumes of fountain grass,
Pennisetum alopecuroides, are
highlighted by the sun.

>> *Wings of Morning*, by
Marshall Fredericks,
enhances the outdoor
patio of the Taste of
the Gardens Café.

in the open branches of maples,
the closed hand of the oak's leaves.
Even the roots—those tender dreamers that live
their invisible lives in total darkness—
can feel a new day begin. Nothing tentative
about vibrant birdsong announcing the dew
as crystal gemstones on blades
of wild grass. Nothing tentative about the vast
expanse of sky constantly redefining the idea
of blue, redefining our idea of ourselves—
children of the earth surrounded by all shades
of green: bud and forest, stem and meadow.
The color that begins each day with the thin song
of memory, the awakened dream of gossamer,
our imagined lives waiting to be lived.

A Masterpiece in Process
1990–2005

1990
The West Michigan Horticultural Society approaches Frederik Meijer about donating a parcel of land, owned by Meijer Inc, as a potential home for the Gardens.

January 1991
Meijer Inc offers 70.7 acres of land in Grand Rapids Township for the Gardens site. Frederik Meijer donates his collection of sculpture by celebrated American sculptor Marshall Fredericks.

April 20, 1995
Frederik Meijer Gardens opens to the public with the Lena Meijer Conservatory, a 15,000-square-foot glass house with tropical plants from five continents; the DeVos Family Gift Shop; the café; the Hoffman Family Auditorium; the Peter M. Wege Library; and the Hauenstein and Pfeiffer meeting rooms.

September 22, 1995
The Victorian Garden opens, re-creating a conservatory typically found in private homes of the late 1800s.

1996
A sculpture advisory committee comprising visual arts professionals, collectors, academics, and Meijer Foundation counsel is appointed to oversee the building of a significant sculpture collection.

January 20, 1996
The Earl & Donnalee Holton Arid Garden opens. It comprises plants from arid climates of the world, including Africa and North, Central, and South America.

September 1997
The Leslie E. Tassell English Perennial & Bulb Garden opens, created by renowned English garden designer Penelope Hobhouse and James van Sweden.

April 1998
The Gardens kicks off a $12.8 million expansion campaign, to include the addition of a boulevard entrance, a new multipurpose 800-seat auditorium, interior galleries for sculpture exhibitions, classrooms, and more parking.

April 19, 1999
The Gardens welcomes its one-millionth visitor, 8-year-old Adam Abbott of Wayland, Michigan.

| 1990–1994 | 1995 | 1996 | 1997 | 1998 | 1999 |

June 1992
A community campaign kicks off to raise $13.1 million to build the Gardens.

August 1993
Groundbreaking takes place. Construction begins immediately.

March 1994
The Michigan Botanic Garden is renamed Frederik Meijer Gardens after its major benefactor.

October 15, 1995
The Wege Nature Trail and Frey Boardwalk open.

November 17, 1995
The Gardener's Corner Gift Shop opens, featuring plants, gardening tools, horticultural supplies, and books.

November 23–December 31, 1995
Christmas Around the World debuts, the first exhibit that will become a Gardens' annual event. Created by community volunteers Starr Meijer and Meg Miller Willit, it features holiday trees and traditions from around the world.

February 14–March 15, 1996
Butterflies Are Blooming debuts, the Gardens' second exhibit to be held annually. Fifty thousand visitors flock to see thousands of tropical butterflies fly free in the Lena Meijer Conservatory.

September 1996
The Jennifer C. Groot New American Garden opens, designed by internationally known landscape designer James van Sweden.

December 1996
The Grace Jarecki Seasonal Display Greenhouse opens, featuring indoor seasonal displays of plants and flowers.

October 1997
The sculpture collection grows to 84 works by internationally known artists.

June 1998
The Gwen Frostic Woodland Shade Garden opens along the Wege Nature Trail. Dedicated to the popular Michigan artist, it includes rhododendrons, azaleas, and shade perennials.

July–August 1999
Three significant sculptures are acquired and installed along a new one-half-mile-long sculpture trail that will become a footprint for the future Sculpture Park: *Cabin Creek* by Deborah Butterfield, *Aria* by Alexander Liberman, and *Full Circle* by Carolyn Ottmers.

October 7, 1999
The American Horse, by Nina Akamu, is unveiled in the DeVos Van Andel Piazza before an audience of 4,800 guests. The 24-foot-tall sculpture is Akamu's homage to a never-completed design by Leonardo da Vinci.

April 2000
Eve, a major work by French master Auguste Rodin, is acquired. Later this year, the Gardens acquires sculpture by Antony Gormley, Dietrich Klinge, Jacques Lipchitz, Aristide Maillol, Henry Moore, and Arnaldo Pomodoro.

September 2000
The Phase II expansion opens, more than doubling the indoor space; increasing facility rental potential; and providing new areas for sculpture exhibitions, gift shopping, guest dining, educational programs, and improved visitor services. Two exhibitions premiere in the new sculpture galleries: *Richard Hunt: American Visionary* and *Imaging the Divine: Religious and Spiritual Themes of Marshall Fredericks.*

September 2001
The Arthur and Elizabeth Snell Sculpture Center, an orientation and discovery space, opens. It provides educational and interpretive information to help visitors appreciate sculpture from different perspectives including style, creative decision-making, inspiration, and process.

October 27, 2001
The Kenneth E. Nelson Carnivorous Plant House, one of the largest and finest carnivorous plant collections in the United States, opens.

January–March 2002
The exhibition *Rodin: Gates of Hell* takes place in the indoor galleries.

Frederik Meijer Gardens is renamed Frederik Meijer Gardens & Sculpture Park.

May 16, 2002
The 30-acre Sculpture Park opens to the public. The aesthetic experience of 24 works by Abakanowicz, di Suvero, Gormley, Maillol, Moore, Pomodoro, Rickey, and other internationally celebrated artists is informed and enhanced by waterfalls, streams, woodlands, wildflowers, and grassy meadows.

January–May 2003
Chihuly at the Gardens, featuring glass works by Dale Chihuly, becomes the most popular temporary sculpture exhibition to date.

May 17, 2003
Michigan's Farm Garden opens, a place where visitors can experience heirloom vegetable gardens, orchards, and farm animal sculptures in a whimsical barnyard setting. The Farm includes a three-quarter-scale replica of Lena Rader Meijer's childhood home and an authentic 100-year-old barn and windmill.

January–May 2004
George Segal: America debuts, the first exhibition in 40 years of work by this renowned American sculptor.

June 20, 2004
The Lena Meijer Children's Garden, one of the largest interactive children's gardens in the nation, opens with 10 thematic areas: Kid-Sense Garden, Great Lakes Garden, Story-Telling Garden, Rock Quarry, Log Cabin, Treehouse Village, Butterfly Maze, Woodland Wetland, Labyrinth, and Sculpture Walk.

January–May 2005
The exhibition *Henry Moore: Imaginary Landscapes* takes place. The Gardens is the only North American venue to exhibit this collection of Moore's work from the Henry Moore Foundation.

2000	2001	2002	2003	2004	2005

October 2000
Richard Hunt's *Column of the Free Spirit,* the first large-scale work commissioned for the Sculpture Park, is unveiled.

December 2000
A new work by Magdalena Abakanowicz is added to the sculpture collection.

December 2001
Membership exceeds 10,000 households.

The sculpture collection grows in breadth with works by Jim Dine, Mark di Suvero, Keith Haring, Barbara Hepworth, Henry Moore, Louise Nevelson, and George Rickey.

August 14, 2002
The Gardens welcomes its two-millionth visitor, 4-year-old Jamie Lynn Urban of Ada, Michigan.

December 2002
New sculpture is added to the collection throughout the year including work by Roy Lichtenstein, Igor Mitoraj, Juan Muñoz, Claes Oldenburg and Coosje van Bruggen, Mimmo Paladino, and George Segal.

June 15, 2003
The new 1,600-seat outdoor amphitheater opens with a concert by musician Art Garfunkel.

December 2003
The sculpture collection continues to flourish with the addition of works by Arman, Hanneke Beaumont, Louise Bourgeois, Lynn Chadwick, Dale Chihuly, Barry Flannigan, Henri Laurens, and Auguste Rodin.

October 21, 2004
The Gardens welcomes its three-millionth visitor, Judy Dodd of Claremont, California.

December 2004
New sculpture added to the collection throughout the year includes the work of Chakaia Booker, Anthony Caro, Edgar Degas, Michele Oka Doner, and Bernar Venet.

Volunteers contributed 473,091 hours of service to the Gardens in its first decade from 1995 through 2004.

April 20, 2005
Frederik Meijer Gardens & Sculpture Park celebrates 10 years of growth with a gala event for donors, volunteers, and key supporters who helped the Gardens achieve acclaim as one of the largest, most innovative cultural institutions in the Midwest.

Contributors

WILLIAM J. HEBERT is a photojournalist and a commercial photographer who has spent years traveling throughout the world with his camera. His work has appeared in numerous publications, including *Newsweek* and *National Geographic,* and he has photographed for the American Cancer Society, Herman Miller, Steelcase, and United Airlines. Many of his images are featured as stock photographs on national Web sites. In 2003, he won a national Addy® Award in the world's largest advertising competition.

ALAN ROSAS has been a writer and art director for more than twenty years. He is the founder of Ambitec Incorporated, an award-winning communications company with global clients. His most critically acclaimed projects are about art, architecture, and history, including *Renewing of a Vision,* a video history on the restoration of Frank Lloyd Wright's Meyer May house in Grand Rapids, Michigan, and *A Place Where Promises Are Kept,* a history film about the Heinz Corporation.

PATRICIA CLARK is a professor in the Writing Department and Poet-in-Residence at Grand Valley State University in Allendale, Michigan. Her published works include two books of poetry: *My Father on a Bicycle* and *North of Wondering.* She also co-edited an anthology of women writers, *Worlds in Our Words.* Her work has appeared in *The Atlantic Monthly, New England Review, North American Review, Pennsylvania Review, Poetry, Slate,* and *Stand.* Honors include the Lucille Medwick Memorial Award from the Poetry Society of America; the *Mississippi Review* Poetry Award; and residencies at the MacDowell Colony, the Ragdale Foundation, the Tyrone Guthrie Centre, and the Virginia Center for the Arts.

LINDA NEMEC FOSTER was chosen to be the first poet laureate of Grand Rapids, Michigan, by the Humanities Council in 2003. She has taught poetry workshops for the Michigan Council for the Arts since 1980. She is the author of six collections of poetry. *Living in the Fire Nest* was a finalist for the Poet's Prize sponsored by the Nicholas Roerich Museum, New York City, and *Amber Necklace from Gdansk* was a finalist for the Ohio Book Award in poetry. Her work has appeared in *The Georgia Review, Indiana Review, Mid-American Review, New American Writing, Nimrod, North American Review, Quarterly West,* and other literary publications. Foster's poems have been translated in Europe, produced for the stage in Detroit, and included in art exhibitions in the Midwest and New York. She has received awards for her poetry from the National Writer's Voice Project and the Academy of American poets, among others. Recently, she was a featured author on *New Letters on the Air,* a nationally syndicated radio show produced by National Public Radio.

DAN GERBER has published several collections of poems, including *A Last Bridge Home: New and Selected Poems;* a volume of selected essays called *A Second Life;* a collection of short stories titled *Grass Fires;* three novels, including *A Voice from the River;* and a book on the Indianapolis 500. His work has received two Push Cart nominations and was selected for Best American Poetry 1999. He also received *Foreword Magazine*'s 1999 Gold Medal Book of the Year Award in poetry for *Trying to Catch the Horses,* the Michigan Author Award in 1992, and the Mark Twain Award in 2001.

MIRIAM PEDERSON is an associate professor of English at Aquinas College in Grand Rapids, Michigan. She is the author of a chapbook called *This Brief Light.* Her poetry has been published in many anthologies, journals, and small press magazines including *The Book of Birth Poetry, Christianity and Literature, Kalliope, The McGuffin, New Poems from the Third Coast: Contemporary Michigan Poetry, Passages North, Poets On,* and *Sing, Heavenly Muse.* Her poems, in collaboration with sculpture created by her husband, Ron Pederson, are exhibited in regional galleries in the Midwest.

RODNEY TORRESON has taught for many years at Immanuel–St. James Lutheran School in Grand Rapids, Michigan, where his students have been consistent winners in the annual Kent County Poetry Contest. His own work has appeared in *Beloit Poetry Journal, Kansas Quarterly,* and *The New York Quarterly.* His publications include a chapbook, *On a Moonstruck Gravel Road,* and two collections of poems, *The Ripening of Pinstripes: Called-Shots on the New York Yankees* and *A Breathable Light.*

ROBERT VANDERMOLEN is the author of eight collections and two chapbooks of poetry, including *Along the River, Circumstances,* and *Of Pines.* His most recent volume of verse is *Breath.* In addition to writing poetry, he has reviewed books, was poetry editor for the *Michigan Sports Gazette,* literary editor for the Newaygo County (Michigan) Council for the Arts newsletter, and taught English at Grand Rapids Community College. He is currently a member of the Grand Rapids Historical Commission.

Acknowledgments

Frederik Meijer Gardens & Sculpture Park gratefully acknowledges the following individuals who generously contributed their talents to the creation of this anniversary book:

> Patricia Clark
> Linda Nemec Foster
> Dan Gerber
> William J. Hebert
> Miriam Pederson
> Alan Rosas
> Rodney Torreson
> Robert VanderMolen

We would also like to acknowledge the collaborative efforts of those who helped make this publication possible:

> E. Jane Connell, Fine Arts Services, Manlius, New York

> Ed Marquand, Marie Weiler, and Jeff Wincapaw, Marquand Books, Inc., Seattle

> Joseph Antenucci Becherer, Jeannie Becker, Dennis Bowman, R. Brent Dennis, Lucinda Grover, Dawn Kibben, Steven LaWarre, Diane Mangnuson, Robert McCartney, Carolyn Miller, K.C. Mitchell, Joseph Moleski, Stacie Niedzwiecki, Kimberly Pant, Marlene Seida, Chris Smith, Linda Thompson, Marlene Vanderhill, Melissa Van Uffelen, Ken Wenger, and Sally Littlefair Zarafonetis, Frederik Meijer Gardens & Sculpture Park

In addition, we thank the artists and donors who have provided the rights that allow for the reproductions of sculpture herein.

We offer a very sincere thank-you to all our members and donors, as well as to the hundreds of volunteers who have dedicated their time and resources to help make the Gardens the special place that it has become.

Finally, we would like to express our appreciation to the Meijer Foundation for its generous support and, most of all, to Fred and Lena Meijer for their dream of bringing horticulture and sculpture together for the enjoyment of people from all walks of life.

Works of Art Illustrated

Page 3: *middle ground:* Magdalena Abakanowicz (Polish, born 1930), *The Skulls,* temporary outdoor exhibition, October 2002–September 2004. © Magdalena Abakanowicz

Page 9: Dietrich Klinge (German, born 1954), *Grosser Trefree,* 2000; bronze, 4/6 (fourth in an edition of six), H. 56¾ inches (144 cm); Gift of Fred and Lena Meijer, 2001.10. © 2002 Dietrich Klinge

Page 12: Alexander Liberman (American, born Russia, 1912–1999), *Aria* (detail), 1979–1983; painted steel, H. 42 feet (1280.2 cm); Gift of Fred and Lena Meijer, 1999.03. © 2002 Estate of Alexander Liberman

Page 14: *background:* Alexander Liberman, *Aria* (detail), see page 12 above

Page 15: Alexander Liberman, *Aria* (detail), see page 12 above

Page 22: *background:* Joseph Kinnebrew (American, born 1942), *The Visitation: Yea, A Slight Lapse of Purpose, Gifts, Hand Stands,* and *The Majorette,* 1994–1997; cast iron, unique, H. 42 to 69 inches (106.7 to 175.3 cm); Gift of the Hoffius Family in Memory of Barbara C. Hoffius, 1997.07–11. © Joseph Kinnebrew

Page 23: *foreground:* Mimmo Paladino (Italian, born 1948), *Tana,* 1993; bronze, 4/4 (fourth in an edition of four), H. 7 feet, 7 inches (231.1 cm); Gift of Fred and Lena Meijer, 2002.10. © Mimmo Paladino

Page 36: *middle ground:* Magdalena Abakanowicz, *The Skulls,* see page 3 above

Page 37: Hanneke Beaumont (Dutch, born 1947), *Number 26,* 1995–1996; bronze, 6/7 (sixth in an edition seven), H. 5 feet (152.4 cm); Gift of Fred and Lena Meijer, 2002.11. © 1996 Hanneke Beaumont

Page 45: *lower right:* Joseph Kinkel (American, born 1950), *Fred Meijer* (detail), 1998; bronze, unique, H. 48 inches (121.9 cm); Gift of the Meijer Foundation, 1999.01. © 1998 Joseph Kinkel

Page 48: Nina Akamu (American, born 1955), *The American Horse,* 1998; bronze, 2/2 (second in an edition of two), H. 24 feet (731.5 cm); Gift of the Meijer Foundation, 1999.06. © 2002 Leonardo da Vinci's Horse, Inc.

Page 58: *background:* Marshall Fredericks (American, 1908–1998), *Frog,* 1995; bronze, H. 6 feet (182.9 cm); Gift of Fred and Lena Meijer, 1995.12. © Marshall Fredericks

Page 68: Mark di Suvero (American, born 1933), *Scarlatti,* 1994–2000; steel, H. 25 feet, 4 inches (772.2 cm); Gift of Fred and Lena Meijer, 2001.14. © Mark di Suvero

Page 69: Arnaldo Pomodoro (Italian, born 1926), *Disk in the Form of a Desert Rose,* 1993–1994, Meijer Sculpture Park cast, 1999–2000; bronze, 2/2 (second in an edition of two), DIAM. 9 feet, 11 inches (302.3 cm); Gift of Fred and Lena Meijer, 2000.09. © Arnaldo Pomodoro

Page 70: *background, right image:* George Rickey (American, born 1907), *Four Open Squares Horizontal Gyratory—Tapered* (detail), 1984; stainless steel, 2/3 (second in an edition of three), H. 16½ inches (41.9 cm) above water; Gift of Fred and Lena Meijer, 2001.07. Art © Estate of George Rickey/Licensed by VAGA, New York, NY

Page 71: Auguste Rodin (French, 1840–1917), *Eve* (detail), 1881 (model), Meijer Sculpture Park cast, before 1920; bronze, H. 68½ inches (174 cm); Gift of Fred and Lena Meijer, 2000.11

Page 73: George Rickey, *Four Open Squares Horizontal Gyratory—Tapered,* see page 70 above

Page 77: Dale Chihuly (American, born 1941), *Gilded Champagne Gardens Chandelier* (detail), 2003; glass, H. 14 feet, 1 inch (429.3 cm); Gift of Jack H. Miller and Fred and Lena Meijer, 2003.01. © 2003 Dale Chihuly

Page 79: *foreground:* Leonard Streckfus (American, b. 1951), *Wolf Family* (detail), 2004; fabricated metals, H. 27 to 35 inches (68.6 to 88.9 cm); Gift of Fred and Lena Meijer, 2004.03. © 2004 Leonard Streckfus. *background:* Marshall Fredericks (American, 1908–1998), *Three Clowns* (detail), 1938, Meijer Sculpture Park cast, 1991; bronze, H. 10 to 12 feet (304.8 to 365.8 cm); Gift of Fred and Lena Meijer, 1995.05–07. © Marshall Fredericks

Page 81: Auguste Rodin, *Eve,* see page 71 above

Page 84: Deborah Butterfield (American, born 1949), *Cabin Creek,* 1999; bronze, unique, H. 88 inches (223.5 cm); Gift of Fred and Lena Meijer, 1999.02. © Deborah Butterfield

Page 85: George Rickey, *Four Open Squares Horizontal Gyratory—Tapered,* see page 70 above

Page 86: Nina Akamu, *The American Horse,* see page 48 above

Page 92: *background:* Alexander Liberman, *Aria* (detail), see page 12 above

Page 95: *left:* Claes Oldenburg (American, born Sweden, 1929) and Coosje van Bruggen (American, born the Netherlands, 1942), *Plantoir* (detail), 2001; stainless steel, aluminum, and fiberglass, painted, AP/3 (artist's proof for an edition of three), H. 23 feet, 11 inches (729 cm); Gift of Fred and Lena Meijer, 2002.1. © Claes Oldenburg and Coosje van Bruggen

Page 97: Dietrich Klinge, *Grosser Trefree,* see page 9 above

Page 100: Marshall Fredericks (American, 1908–1998), *Wings of Morning,* 1987; Meijer Sculpture Park cast, 1995; bronze, H. 8 feet (243.8 cm); Gift of Fred and Lena Meijer, 1995.27. © Marshall Fredericks